A Crisis of Evil

Spiritual Warfare in Our Midst

Dedication

"This book is dedicated to all the warriors who are doing their best to fight evil wherever and whenever they encounter it. Put on the armor of God and keep up the fight."

A Crisis of Evil

Spiritual Warfare in our Midst

"The Only Thing Necessary for the Triumph of Evil is for Good Men to do nothing."

Edmund Burke

Introduction

We are living in perilous times where the dark is attempting to overtake the light. Evil is attempting to triumph over good, and sadly too many people don't even seem to realize they are part of the process. Think about the numerous things today that were considered unacceptable just a short time ago and today they are accepted without question. The New World Encyclopedia defines evil as anything that brings about harm, painful and unpleasant effects, in this book we will look at some of those things. There will be some readers that may be offended by what is said here and that is understandable because, in many cases, people have their way of defining evil. I ask that you keep an open mind as you read these chapters.

Can you think of some examples that would fit the definition? How about the amount of sex and violence on television and movies? In your opinion, is same-sex marriage acceptable? How about the legalization or decriminalization of marijuana, does that benefit our society in any way? Abortion is a very sensitive subject for many people; some believe it is a woman's right to choose what she does with her body. Other people believe that aborting a fetus regardless of age is an unlawful killing, what do you think? Studies of the occult and Satanism have increased significantly in recent years, and people are abandoning anything related to

Jesus Christ. These are just a few issues that have become commonplace in our society today.

Here are some questions to consider: can we honestly say that allowing these types of things to become part of our lives has improved the quality of life for us and our children? Do you enjoy watching movies and television more today than you used to or are you more concerned about what you are watching and what your children may see right in your home? Do you believe your children will have a better life than you have had so far or are they destined to battle evil their whole lives? In Isaiah 5:20 we read, "Woe unto them that call evil good, and good evil; that put darkness for light, and light for darkness; that put bitter for sweet, and sweet for bitter."

Today we see the words of this scripture occurring daily. We see the entertainment industry portraying lust, deceit, and pornography as things that are not only good because that is the way the world is, but things that should be emulated by young people. There are people today who do not believe in God, they believe that everything is the result of their personal efforts, and that is what Satan is promoting. These individuals firmly believe that the end justifies the means regardless of who or what is affected.

Here is something you may be familiar with, there used to be a time when profanity in a person's language was the exception and used by only a few people. Today's younger generation has adopted profanity as a valid form of communication. Most of the people that have adopted this language don't seem to understand that they are simply demonstrating ignorance and lack of vocabulary to express themselves when they use profanity in conversation.

The media is playing a major role in the proliferation of evil also. In the interest of ratings and profits, they have become complicit in promoting debauchery through the use of television and the internet. The internet has become one of Satan's favorite tools to reach the masses of people that are weak and don't believe in God. Think about what you have seen on television or the internet just in the last few days?

In this book, an attempt will be made to bring about some awareness of the various types of evil that we are all facing every day and the reasons for their existence. Think about your life and the lives of those you love, what can you do to protect yourself and them? Consider what you want for your future; will these evil elements be part of that future? More importantly, if you feel you need to make changes to what is going on around you, don't wait, make those changes now.

There are reasons why these things are taking place. Some people agree with these reasons, and other people don't, you will have to make up your mind. The fact is that it doesn't matter whether you agree or not, because all of the things that will be brought out in this book are happening now, and that is just the way it is.

Many of the issues you read about may be ones that you many not even recognize as being evil. Every effort will be made to provide you with enough information so that you can understand why the issue is an evil item. Some of the issues are obvious, for example, violence against others, drugs, alcohol and hatred of others.

There will be Biblical references, where appropriate, to illustrate some of the points in the book. I would like to courage you, as the reader, to seek out additional information in your Bible.

Chapter One

Loss of Moral Compass

Before we begin this discussion let us understand what moral compass is by looking at a definition: *Moral Compass is a natural feeling that makes people know what is right and what is wrong and how to behave.* (Cambridge Dictionary)

A recent study done at Notre Dame University points out that young people may not be doing anything worse than they have always done between the ages of eighteen and twenty-three. What is disturbing is the way they are talking and thinking about moral issues. Many of the people in the study could not provide any example of what a moral dilemma was, much less how to deal with one. One respondent answered this way: "I don't deal with right and wrong." They agreed that rape and murder were wrong, but not so much when it came to drunk driving, cheating in school, or cheating on a partner.

So why is it that we see this happening in our society? Primarily it is happening because, as a nation, we have gotten away from the core values upon which our nation was built. There was a time in this country when people shook hands and gave their word, and that was as good as any contract. Not so today, many people do not even know what it means to, "Give your word," much less keep it. We have removed elements like the Ten Commandments from our schools, courthouses, and other public buildings. These guiding principles upon which our countries laws were based are no longer seen outside of a church, and even some churches no longer display them.

You will hear people who don't believe in God say, "Oh, those are just a bunch of meaningless words, and who knows who wrote them anyway." These are the very words that are used to base some of our most important laws, such as, "Thou shall not kill," and "Thou shall not steal." There are many other laws that are based on the Ten Commandments if a person just bothers to look. If you have not read the Ten Commandments in a while, this might be a good time to refresh your memory.

Another reason young people have lost their moral compass is because no one bother to teach them the true difference between right and wrong, or what it means to do the right thing. Parents today are so preoccupied with their self-gratification that they neglect the upbringing of their children. They send the child off to school and expect the teachers to explain to the child these differences, and when the child behaves in a manner that is wrong, they blame the teacher. The parents abdicate their responsibilities to teach the children about right and wrong.

Having said that, let us not delude ourselves; young people are not the only ones who have lost their way. Many adults today feel there is nothing wrong with doing whatever it takes to get ahead, regardless of who gets hurt in the process. It is, after all, a dog eat dog world out there, and everyone does what is necessary to survive. They cheat; they steal, and they gossip. They do anything necessary to show that they are better than the next person and deserve recognition. If and when they have children, they pass these attitudes on to them.

The truth is we have gotten away from all the things that made our country great in the first place. Not even, our politicians can get along and work together for the best interest of the people anymore. Today's legislators are more interested in getting re-elected and keeping their political perks, than in doing what is right for the people that elected them. Our U.S. Supreme Court is now so divided that laws that they decide upon leave people wondering why we even have such a court. So, it is no surprise when young people ask, "What is a moral compass?"

How many times have you heard the phrase, "If it feels good, do it,"? This phrase has been responsible for many people taking the words and engaging in whatever behavior they desire, no matter if it is evil and hurts someone. People of all ages ascribe to this philosophy, although young people seem to be most influenced by this concept. For example, as adults, we all know that it is against the law to drive under the influence of drugs or alcohol; it is simply a right or wrong thing to do. Many young people say, "Oh it's okay if I drive I'm only a little buzzed; besides I don't have to go far." The reality, of course, is that this is the wrong thing to do and could lead to injury or death.

The one activity that seems to remain constant among both older and younger people is that adultery for married people is still wrong. There is a bit of a paradox her because, in the dating world, there appears to be an expectation that having sex is part of the date. Even on television, in programs such as the Bachelor, a man is presented with a harem of women to choose from based on his subjective evaluation of their performance, which may include sexual behavior.

There was once a time in our country when a person's word was their bond. People would even enter into legal contracts based on a handshake and their given word. Today, a person's word means little to nothing; agreements are entered into by iron-clad written legal documents enforceable in courts of law. Not only do strangers sue each other, but even family members sue each other, simply because they no longer trust each other to do what they say they will do. The levels of selfishness among individuals have reached unprecedented levels.

People in many walks of life have lost any semblance of integrity, and this includes business people and politicians. Just look at what happened during the recent housing crisis. Bankers knew the loans they were making to some people were bad loans and that the people would ultimately default on those loans, but they did not care because there was a profit in the transaction. They had no empathy for the families that would be impacted by the banks lack of integrity.

Our divorce rate continues to soar because people are no longer willing to honor their commitments. During the wedding ceremony, we listen to the happy couple pledge their undying love for each other till death do they part. A short time later, they are both talking to their respective lawyers, pontificating their hatred for the same person they had earlier pledged eternal love.

Much of what we see happening in this loss of moral compass comes from a lack of example. When children are growing up, they tend to imitate what they see and hear from their parents or caregivers. If those examples are positive, that is what they will mimic, conversely if those examples are negative, then, it is no surprise that they will imitate those negative behaviors. Parents must take on the responsibility of teaching their children right from wrong and demonstrating the correct behaviors for the child to emulate.

Obviously, not everyone is a Christian, and even some so-called Christians are untrustworthy. Christians do tend to have a more solid moral compass then those who are not believers. Christians believe in the teachings of Jesus Christ and try to model their behavior based on the principles given in the Holy Bible. Christians believe in helping others, in keeping their word, in respecting people and property and in telling the truth. I grew up in this way and I still support and live by all those ideas.

If you feel you have lost your moral compass, now is a good time to reassess yourself. Start by abiding in the "Golden Rule," do unto others as you would have them do unto you. A great place to begin again to reset your moral compass is by living the golden rule. Keep in mind this only a beginning, a place to start. Like many other changes we make in life, start by making small changes. For example, promise yourself you will not tell a single lie today. Can you do it? Some people simply cannot go a whole day without telling a lie, such a small thing. Are you falling prey to that behavior? What other things are you doing that are pushing you in the wrong direction?

Chapter Two

The Role of the Media

Whether you realize it or not the media is influencing everything that you do in your life. From the toothpaste, you used this morning to what you have for dinner tonight. Through the use of advertising, on television, radio, the internet, your cell phone, billboards and every other type of medium out there the media promotes everything, good and bad.

Today you see advertising for just about any product you can think of, from baby food to condoms or where to get a vasectomy. The media promotes a variety of movies; some family oriented and some not. Most carry a restricted rating because of language, violence and sexually explicit scenes including forcible rape. You are subjected to all this every day, and so are your children.

People are surprised when a child manages to obtain one or more guns and goes out to commit some act of violence against someone else. It happened at Columbine, and it has happened in many other places including Sandy Hook Elementary School, where innocent children were killed for no reason. We should not be surprised or alarmed when these things happen because we are allowing the media to promote this type of behavior to our children. Through the proliferation of violent video games and movies, children see this behavior and internalize it as something that is not only acceptable, but something that can be claimed as a badge of honor. They want to be like those characters on the screen, with the glamorous lifestyle, always getting the best of everything and not being held accountable for their actions.

Sadly, parents, in many cases, are not helping either because they allow children to watch all this junk and to act disrespectfully to police, teachers and elders. When the child gets into trouble, these same parents place the blame on someone else for not taking care of the problem, most of the time these are teachers. The truth, of course, lies in the fact that the parents have been negligent in instructing the child on how they should behavior in a civilized society and they have failed to instill proper values and discipline.

For many years, the media has allowed the proliferation of immorality through the numerous pornographic sites that exist on the internet. Pornography is a multi-billion dollar business, and there are thousands, if not millions, of companies that are exploiting this market. Just about every conceivable type of perversion is found on the internet. Additionally, there are individuals on many of those sites that are promoting themselves as being willing participants in all of these perverted activities and claiming they are fun, and the viewer should consider doing it also. There are millions of these sites available to anyone, young or old; it makes no difference. Many of these sites are free, and others charge a fee, but even those that are free are making money on advertising a variety of products, from condoms to Viagra.

The media has become Satan's greatest tool to corrupt the children of God, and too many people are falling right into the trap. Guess what? Satan will steal your children away from you if you let him. How many times in the last few years have we heard in school shooting incidents, "I don't understand it, he was such a good boy." When the child's computer is examined by police, there is evidence in the machine that shows the child was visiting all types of sites promoting violence against other people and how to go about making it happen. Where were the parents? Who was monitoring what this child was viewing? Satan and his demons, they were there.

In John 2-10 we read: "If someone comes to your meeting and does not teach the truth about Christ, don't invite him to your house or encourage him in any way. Anyone who encourages him becomes a partner in his evil work." Have you become a partner in the evil work of the media whom you have invited into your home every day?

It is critically important that we take another look at whom and what we are allowing to come into our home through the use of the media. Remember, Satan thrives on the sin of vanity, and us as human beings with free will tend to fall for this temptation on a regular basis. Guard your heart and your mind from the media and the evil that they put in front of you and your children.

Chapter Three

The Evil of Hate

This behavior is nothing new, people are people, and there are those who hate others simply because they are different than they are and will act to harm them if there is an opportunity. To understand hate, we must understand what the drivers are that cause people to hate others. Many people that are haters become that way because of poor self-esteem or frustration with a particular group or individual. Others want to feel superior or are jealous of those they hate. Others, are fearful of those that are different.

During WWII people in the American government incarcerated thousands of other American citizens simply because they were of German, Japanese or Italian decent. These individuals did nothing wrong. They had been good, law-abiding citizens, but now there was a war on with the peoples of these three countries, and suddenly all of these individuals were viewed as the enemy and supportive of their native countries. There was nothing on which to base this premise, but fear overtook the majority, and since they government represents the majority, these people were incarcerated in camps all over the country. Many of these individuals lost their homes and businesses during the incarceration, and some were even deported to their country of origin, even though they were American citizens. Good people perpetrated evil against their friends and neighbors simply because of fear. We saw similar behavior against Middle Eastern people after the September 11, 2001 attacks.

Once again, this is nothing new, today there are thousands of people in America that hate others because they are African American, Hispanic, Asian, Lesbian, Gay, etc. Don't misunderstand; I do not condone homosexual behavior. I personally believe it is contrary to God's law, but I do not support hate, discrimination and brutality against another human being simply because of their choice of sexual behavior. They will have to sort that one out themselves with the Almighty. We have groups in our country like the Klu Klux Klan, neo-Nazis, Aryan Brotherhood, Mexican Mafia, and many, many others that commit crimes against other people.

There are many areas of the hate spectrum; there are many others that are just as evil. For example, there are individuals that hate others in their families. Not long ago I spoke to a man who has had on ongoing disagreement with his brother for over ten years. They both live in the same city and yet have not spoken to each other in all that time. When I asked him what the dispute was about, it turned out is was over a loan of one hundred dollars which the brother had failed to repay. It is hard to imagine that two grown men, both now near middle age have essentially destroyed a family relationship over a mere hundred dollars. Satan wants people like these men, to turn on each other, breaking the bond of love between them is a victory for the devil.

Sadly, we continue to see teenagers develop feelings of hate towards their parents. Some of these feelings are justifiable when the parent turns their back on those children in favor of self-gratification. Other times these children fall prey to the influences of evil people or messages on the media. Some these young people have become involved in the use of drugs or alcohol and these too are Satan's tools to influence impressionable people.

Lest we ignore the concept of hate in the workplace, it does exist. In the workplace, there are employees that purposely will undermine or sabotage the efforts of another employee to make them look bad or get them fired. People will purposely gossip and makeup stories that are untrue that the employee now has to prove are made up. Because of the nature of these stories, it may be difficult to disprove them and if management believes them the employee is now guilty. It is the worst type of hate because it hides behind the face of righteousness. The recipient of the hatred does not even realize they are the target of some mean-spirited person.

Hate can be one of the worst types of evil in the world, and everyone must guard against it. Satan is always on alert seeking opportunities to convince individuals that they should hate someone else or do something to harm them. It is extremely important for Satan because hate goes contrary to the message that Jesus Christ left behind, which was to love our neighbor as ourselves.

Think about the hate that radical Muslims have adopted towards Jews and Americans. They have taken their holy book, The Quran and selected specific passages that they believe demand that they hate and kill those that they consider are infidels, in order to honor Allah. Just in case you are not aware, there are over one hundred such verses in the Quran that direct Muslims to acts of violence, they can be found in Religion of Peace.com. Satan is probably jumping up and down in joy every time a Muslim takes action against someone based on one of these verses.

Chapter Four

Modern Life and God

The concept of God has always been a primary target for the devil, and our fast paced, modern life has made it even easier to deceive God's people. Many believe that there is no point in believing in God, that He doesn't exist. One of the key arguments is that is God does exist, why does he allow so many bad things to happen to people. What these individuals fail to recognize is that most of the evil that happens in the world is perpetrated by other human beings. People being the way they are and having the free will to act, will always seek someone or something to blame when something evil happens, and if they can't find that, they will always blame God. It is easy to blame God since he never objects to our claim, even if it is totally wrong.

There are those that believe that they descended from apes or even pond scum and that there is no God that created everything. Also, because there is no God, there is no right and wrong; therefore everyone should just do whatever they want to do. Many criminals tend to think this way, and that is why they do what they do. We all have free will, so we should be able to do what we want and should not have to worry about being held accountable right? Wrong, this type of thinking could easily lead to anarchy and chaos for everyone.

Positive thinking gurus preach that because we are intelligent human beings, we can do anything we set our minds to accomplish. The approach sounds great in theory, but not so great in practice. Many parents tell their children they could even be president of the United States, if they wanted to, we know that realistically that is not true. Similar to those parents that tell their children that they can be sports stars, the odds are highly unlikely. The people of Babel in the Bible thought they could build a structure to reach heaven until God confused their language, and that was the end of that story. Positive thinking can be a good thing provided we don't leave God out of the equation and recognize that it is God first, above all, things. Atheists claim they don't believe in God and yet in not believing they confirm His existence.

Our modern world has brought us from one conflict to another where people find themselves in states of war. Thousands of people lose their lives in the interest of political ends designed by evil men. We can look at the Iraq conflict as a prime example. Evil men in leadership positions in the United States government orchestrated this conflict under false pretenses to further their political gains. Claims made were that the government of

Iraq was responsible for the September 11, 2001 terrorist events and that they possessed weapons of mass destruction in Iraq. No weapons were ever found, and not one of the individuals involved in the terrorist attacks was an Iraqi.

We as a nation are technically superior to any other generation prior to ours. This technology has allowed us to have access to information at the click of a mouse or a tap on smart-phone. Unfortunately, this information includes every conceivable type of perversion known to man. There are thousands of evil people in the world who are taking advantage of the weaknesses of human beings and the available technology. The technology provides access to all the perverted information a person can imagine.

Everything from child pornography to bomb making and even germ warfare are available to anyone who cares to search for them. Sadly, this type of evil information is available from the comfort of a person's home. Child pornographers, for example, use this same information super highway to transmit and build their criminal empires, hurting thousands in the process.

The modern life technology is truly a double-edged sword. While it certainly has a propensity for good, there is so much evil that is being sent over those communications channels and millions of people are the victims. Make no mistake, every time you turn on your computer, Satan, and his demons will be there to tempt you to go places you know are wrong. Computer temptation applies not only to you, but to your loved ones also, including your children. Please, be mindful of the hazards of this modern life and always look to Jesus Christ for guidance.

Chapter Five

Older People and Children, Targets of Evil

Older people and young children are similar when it concerns the evil that victimizes these individuals. Whether it is actual physical abuse or mental/emotional abuse, both of these groups are vulnerable targets for predators. You may wonder how an older person can be physically abused. Sadly, it happens in nursing homes every day by those same people that are hired to take care of them. Leaving a person that cannot do for themselves sitting in their waste for example, or not giving them water when they are thirsty. These are just some examples of physical abuse experienced by the elderly; there are many others. Every year there are thousands of these senior citizens that are abused or exploited by those who should know better. These are individuals, who through no fault of their own, have become unable to care for themselves or defend themselves against unscrupulous, evil people. This physical abuse can also include: slapping, restraining and even using drugs to make them sleep. Perhaps a form of abuse that is all too common but seldom talked about is the issue of abandonment. Too many adults tend to abandon their parents.

Too many adults abandon their parents when those people get older. They move away from home, maybe to another city or even another state. Initially, there may be a phone call or two, but they become less and less. Once it gets to the point where the older parent is having difficulty taking care of themselves, the children put them into a nursing home and essentially, forget about them until they die. I suspect that many of you reading have seen this happen.

In days of old, elders were taken in by family members and they remained surrounded by loved ones, where they passed on their wisdom and knowledge to the next generation. They remained with the family until it was time for them to pass on with dignity, not alone, surrounded by strangers, which is what happens in a nursing home. Today, many modern families will not even consider taking in an older person, claiming they are too much of burden and that they could not give them adequate care. As if that is what they get in a nursing home.

In my opinion, there is no greater sin against God and humanity than to abuse and exploit children. There are numerous countries in the world today where children are a commodity to be bought and sold, or they are a useless nuisance. A few days ago a news story broke in Las Vegas, NV where a husband, wife, and ex-wife were sexually abusing their children, filming despicable acts and selling the footage to an internet pornographer. These evil people were committing these atrocities against their flesh and blood, in their home and had been doing it for years. The victims ranged in age from five to their late teens. These adults believed that because these were their children, they had the right to do whatever they wanted to with them.

How could people perpetrate such evil? Our society is the one we have allowed to evolve over the last several decades. Our permissiveness allows evil to be accepted as good. By allowing pornography to proliferate; by becoming numb to what we watch on television and by not monitoring what we and our family view on the internet, evil has made its way into our homes. As a result, that evil is hardly recognized anymore, and it has become okay for it to be in our midst.

Simply because they are children does not give an adult permission to abuse or exploit a child. Many third world countries use children to perform labor for meager wages or even no wages; this too is a form or evil. Here in the United States, many retail corporations buy and market products that are made by these children, so, in an indirect way, they are facilitating the exploitation of these children too. Once again, we see adults exploiting children and perpetrating evil for the simple motive of profit.

Perhaps the worst of this exploitation is in the sex industry where many Asian countries allow child pornography and facilitate sexual abuse of children by adults. Some of these countries even advertise "sexual vacations," for adults that want to have sex with children. Major news networks have done news stories on these types of sex vacations to Thailand and Indonesia. The sex trade is a multi-billion dollar industry, and the use of children is just a part of that trade

Chapter Six

Lack of Respect for Human Life

Today we live in a world that is much different from even just a short twenty years ago. All you have to do to verify that statement is to watch an episode of the evening news in any large city, and you will get an ear full regarding what evil people are committing against each other. Recently, I saw a news story where a grandfather was walking his grand-daughter who was in a stroller, along a local roadway. A woman who was under the influence of alcohol drove by and hit them with her car. A reasonable person would have stopped to see if she could help or at least call 911; this woman kept on driving and went home. She left the grandfather dead on the side of the road, by some miracle the baby in the stroller survived. The woman is now pending charges; this was not her first time arrested for driving under the influence of alcohol. What kind of evil person does something like this?

It is no secret that there are people in this world that have little, if any, use for people that live in free countries. They have not hesitated to demonstrate that by carrying out the act of terrorism throughout the world. Terrorism is a form of evil that is purposely orchestrated to instill fear in the victims. Obviously terrorists have no respect for human life because they do not care who is killed or maimed by their actions.

There is no shortage of home invasions these days, and that is just another symptom of the lack of respect for others. Not long ago a news item centered on a home invasion where three young men forced their way into the home of an elderly couple. After robbing them, they purposely destroyed valuables and keepsakes. They pistol whipped the old man and put him in the hospital. To add insult to injury, one of the men raped the old woman who was seventy-eight years old. No doubt evil was alive and well during this incident. It is not an uncommon occurrence and happens way too often in larger cities.

Every week we hear about someone being killed, or a body being found somewhere. Overall, there are tens of thousands of people that die from violence somewhere in the world. Crime statistics shows that every twenty-three minutes an American is murdered in this country. What does that say about us as a society?

Perhaps the greatest evil in this area of disrespect for human life is in the area of abortion. According to the Center for Disease Control, in 2011 there were just a little over one million abortions in the United States. About three-fourths of the women undergoing abortions claim that a baby would interfere with their life plans in some way, so they elect to have the fetus terminated.

People argue over the issues surrounding when life begins. Many claim that the fetus is not truly a human being until after thirteen weeks, so pregnancy terminated before that time is not a problem. I believe that the moment that a child is conceived it is a living being and should be accorded the rights of any human being, including protection against termination. People being endowed with free will can justify anything in their mind, no matter how evil or wicked it may be.

Many of you that are reading this know that we have become a society of people who don't get involved. The idea of being our brother's keeper is totally foreign to most individuals and they just want to mind their own business. How many times have you walked by a homeless person, totally ignoring them or even feeling offended because those people are alive? This attitude has resulted in people being assaulted in broad daylight and no one bothering to step in and help. When police arrived and question witnesses people claim they did not see anything, even though they may have information to help catch the offender. Instead they say, "Hey, it's none of my business, why should I stick my nose in it."

The sad truth is that because of this isolationist attitude, people don't help each other anymore. They don't trust each other and don't care to know anything about those around them, not even their neighbors. Do you know your neighbors? When was the last time you helped them out with something? In most small towns, this is not a problem. In large cities that are not the case, places like New York, Los Angeles, Chicago, Houston and San Francisco, people go out of their way not to know their neighbors.

Chapter Seven

The Wickedness of Politics

Some of the most evil acts perpetrated on the people of the United States are done so by those individuals who have been elected to serve those citizens. Today we are still fighting a war in the Middle East that should never have started in the first place. The last Republican administration committed our country to this conflict for simply selfish reason by those in power. Our last president referred to an axis of evil, what he did not say was that the axis of evil included him, the vice-president, and the secretary of defense. These were powerful men who were able to manipulate and intimidate others to follow along with their bidding.

Thousands of Americans have now lost their lives, and tens of thousands of others were injured for a cause that had nothing to do with the security of our country. It was simple greed and vanity on the part of those in power. The situation on September 11, 2001 was publicized by politicians and the media outlets, which they control, that it was necessary for us to get involved in combat in the Middle East. Recent inquiries have determined that the claims made for this involvement were totally false, and we are now so entrenched in that conflict that it will be difficult to extricate ourselves from that nightmare.

There are numerous conspiracy theories out there regarding what happened on September 11, 2001. You may choose to ignore these theories, the choice is yours, but before you do check out what you know for certain about what happened. Who stood to gain the most from such an event? Why would they orchestrate such a thing? I can tell you from first-hand experience that our government is capable of doing just about anything they want to do in the world, and they will find ways to justify doing it. The evil that men do is not limited. Those in high power positions know this all too well and continue to engage in this evil behavior.

Do not misunderstand; I am not singling out any one political party because they are both capable of anything and are both complicit in all sorts of evil perpetrated against their people. Sure they will claim that what they are doing is for the best interested of the country. I served in Vietnam back in the 60's, there was no benefit to any ordinary citizen that I know of, but thousands of politicians and businessmen got filthy rich during that war. The 58,000 men and women who lost their lives and the tens of thousands who were injured, did not benefit one single bit from that event, and now it is being repeated all again in the Middle East.

Many of you are probably aware that rules have changed by the U.S. Supreme Court regarding campaign donations. These changes have resulted in a system where corporations can spend as much money as they feel is necessary to influence a political campaign and essentially buy a politician that will act in the best interest of the donor. When an outside organization fronts the money for the campaign, the individual becomes the indentured servant to that organization for the money they provided. When these people go to Washington, they vote on legislation that is beneficial to the organization, not the citizens who voted for them.

It is not unheard of to destroy a candidate's life and reputation in pursuit of political gain. People that get involved in politics have some admirable goals initially, and their ambition is to make a difference for the people who voted them into office. It does not take long, however before these well-meaning individuals become corrupted by the system. They quickly find out that everything is run by evil people with their personal agendas, and they either fall in line or they are isolated to the point where they can do nothing. Ultimately, their goals become displaced by their thirst and desire for power, and they focus on their ambitions and forget about the common people.

If you have any doubt, take a look back in time, John F. Kennedy and Lyndon Johnson were viewed as great men by most people and they got our country involved in a conflict in Vietnam that resulted in the deaths of over 58,000 Americans and countless wounded. Why? What was the purpose? In the end, the only winners were the big corporations that profited from providing war materials. Richard Nixon left office in disgrace after the Watergate affair in which he was complicit in criminal activity. Bill Clinton dishonored the Office of the President by lying to Congress about his extra-marital shenanigans with Monica Lewinsky and others. Finally, George W. Bush, Dick Cheney, and Donald Rumsfeld got our nation into another money war in the Middle East under the guise of fighting terrorism. We are still trying to extricate ourselves from that one. The main goal here is the profit of big business at the expense of American servicemen's lives.

The last six years have seen an unprecedented division between Republicans and Democrats in the Presidency and the Congress. Much of this division has come from the simple fact that these individuals are fostering their agendas and not the interests of the American people. Many of these individuals have purposely opposed programs proposed by the President that would help the American people, but because the President is from a different political party they have refused to support those programs. The so-called "Tea Party," went into Congress with a mandate that they would oppose everything the President put forth, and they have succeeded to a large extent, at the expense of the American people.

Make no mistake, evil is alive and well in the halls of our great nation and the members of the so-called government, on both sides of the aisle. The makings of a major collapse of our country are already in the making, from the inside out. They will soon become evident to anyone who wishes to open their eyes and see what is going on behind the scenes. If positive change does not occur soon, it will not be long before the United States of America goes the way of the Roman Empire, into oblivion.

Chapter Eight

Or Criminal Justice System in Turmoil

One lonely need look around the court system to see how bad off the system is and much reform is needed. Court dockets are over-loaded, prisons and jails are overcrowded, some large police departments are plagued with corruption and many people have lost respect for the law. To add insult to injury, many States are now either decriminalizing or flat out legalizing the possession and use of marijuana. The primary reason for taking this stance is monetary, one which evil people have seen as a way of lining their pockets regardless of who gets hurt in the process. The people that will get hurt, in this case, are the poor and uneducated, and they will continue to grow and crowd the criminal justice system.

There is no question that the arguments for legalization of marijuana take on a variety of other reasons. Reducing overcrowding of jails, reducing court docket loads and freeing up police to deal with real criminal acts have all been stated. The true question is, who benefits most from this type of decision-making? Primarily the beneficiaries are the producers and distributors of marijuana. Research has shown that the chemical make-up of marijuana impairs brain function, what better way to create a society of mindless humans. If the government allows this behavior, soon we will have a nation of people that don't care about anything other than feeling good and taking substances that provide those feelings. They will be easily controlled and manipulated and will agree to anything, much of that is already happening.

As a nation, we have the largest number of people in prisons and jails of any country in the world. What has happened to our country that requires so many people to be behind bars? Every day in courthouses all over the United States people lose their freedom for violations committed against their fellow man. This behavior follows from the attitudes mentioned in previous chapters of the book and other information that will be presented in later chapters. Today the system of justice is so broken that there does not appear to be a way to fix it. People with significant resources commit serious crimes and manage to get either light sentences or no sentences from the courts. Those with little or no legal resources to help them go to prison and they have no recourse.

Within the last week, two police officers were murdered in cold blood as they sat in their patrol car in New York City. The murderer later shot and killed himself. These officers did not know the shooter, and he did not know them either, he simply killed them because they were in uniform and represented law enforcement. He shot and killed two innocent people and ruined the lives of the two families and brought shame to his family. What kind of an evil mind does it take for a person to do this? It takes a mind that is weak and subject to the influence of Satan and his demons. Please guard your minds, do not allow your mind to be influenced and misled.

In many other criminal cases, we see people committing acts so vile that it leaves us wondering how God could allow such a thing to happen. To add insult to injury, we then see defense attorneys who protect and defend these criminals. Ask anyone of these attorneys why they do it, and they will claim that everyone should be protected under the law and that they are only doing their jobs. Often these criminals will get off and will go out an reoffend again, killing or raping someone. Regardless of what they say, these attorneys are complicit in these second or subsequent criminal acts. I would hate to try to explain to God why I helped a child killer get off, knowing that he was guilty, and later that person killed another child.

The criminal justice system, as broken and in need of reform as it is, is something that we created and continue to allow it to exist. In the last several months, there have been numerous cases of racial tension where African Americans have been killed by Caucasian police officers that were not punished or disciplined by their departments or the courts. This type of activity has fueled racial violence and protests around the country, and it will continue to grow as time goes on because the causes are not being addressed.

The violence that occurs in prisons and jails is not something that is publicized because the media does not have access to those areas and administrators do not publicly report such violence. The truth is that violence inside prisons and jails is common; inmates are stabbed and beaten up every day, sometimes by other inmates, sometimes by staff. In most of these situations there is little accountability, an inmate gets stabbed and dies, an investigation is conducted; no one is found to be guilty because inmates do not rat on each other, so the case is closed, and that is where it ends. Drugs and other contraband are routine funneled into prisons and jails, through visitors, vendors or staff, so the crime continues even inside the institutions.

Chapter Nine

Friends, Neighbors, and Co-workers—A Subtle Evil

We all know people whom we consider good neighbors, friends or co-workers. Today, many of these same people are involved in a variety of evil behaviors that we would never believe they could be involved in, after all they are good people. Over the years, we have all heard stories about mass murderers, in schools, movie theaters or workplaces. When people in the neighborhoods where these people lived are interviewed, they tend to say things like, "He was such a nice guy." In the workplace, after a workplace violence act, the co-workers say, "I would never have believed that he would do something like this."

The truth is that because of the society we live in today, we rarely know our friends, neighbors or co-workers very well. When questioned, people that knew the offender who committed the evil acts don't have anything bad to say about them. Those same people were among them every day.

Child molesters many times are trusted individuals that interact with your children all the time. Parents allow their teenage children to hang out with others that they know nothing about, regarding their backgrounds. Many predators pretend to be younger than they are so they can befriend potential teenage victims. When parents question young people about who their friends are, the child usually reacts by claiming the parent is trying to control them and not allowing them the freedom to be themselves. It must be remembered that children, even teenagers, should not have the same freedom as adults, they should be monitored in their activities and their associations. Children are supposed to be protected by their parents, they must be given guidance and supervision, so it is critical the parents take responsibility for doing these things. When parents fail to do this, there is always someone else out there that is willing to assume the role and take the opportunity to exploit these children.

Sometimes the evil can be much more subtle, such as a neighbor or co-worker spreading rumors and gossip among others that know the person. In the workplace, these rumors can impact the person's employment and in the community gossip can injure a person's reputation with others. Perhaps you have been a victim of such malicious gossip. When this happens to us, we become cynical and distrustful of others, and that is exactly what Satan wants.

Many people are atheists and do not believe in God. They believe that everything that comes their way in life is a result of their personal diligence and skill. They further believe that people that do believe in God are a bunch of mindless fools simply looking for some divine intervention that does not exist. They believe that the Bible is merely an interesting story book written by a bunch of fiction writers at various stages of history. They do not believe in Jesus Christ or any of the miracles he performed. They do not believe in the salvation provided by Jesus because they do not believe in sin.

In modern times, we have seen a proliferation of cults, an unprecedented interest in satanic worship, vampires, werewolves, witches, demons and a variety of unholy behavior. Many people believe in numerous gods and sorcery, and they participate in rituals involving demonology. Think about the movies such as Harry Potter, all based on sorcery and witchcraft, yet parents flock to the theater with their children to see these movies. They buy the DVD's of these movies and many others and bring them into their homes. The Twilight series is all about vampires and werewolves, which are essentially demons and young teenagers, are totally fixated on these movies. These are subtle ways of introduction by Satan to bring people into believing in the occult, which is Satan's playground.

Not only have we seen the increase in acceptance of these evil concepts, but along with them has come deterioration in language. Young people today give little thought to the use of profanity in front of elders and children. There is little respect for the traditional values the country held dear just two generations ago. These too are so-called friends and neighbors.

The acceptance of promiscuous sex and sex out of marriage has become the norm in the dating world, even expected as part of the dating process. Alcohol and substance abuse are continuing to destroy our young people with little restraint being imposed by anyone. The practice of cheating to get what one wants has infected even our military academies and universities. The moral code of our society has degenerated to unprecedented levels.

There was a time in our country when people could count on their friends, neighbors, and co-workers whenever they needed help, that time is now gone. As a matter of fact, in larger cities, people do not even know their neighbors. Many people don't have friends anymore; they may have a few acquaintances, but not friends. In the workplace, co-workers routinely look for instances that they can report to the boss regarding fellow employees. They take these actions in hopes of gaining favor with the boss even though it may hurt someone else. These are all evil acts that have no other purpose than to cause harm to another person.

We hear stories of a tragedy about the person who committed the criminal act and the real truth is that few if anyone, knew the person. They knew bits and pieces about the individual, but they didn't know them. Think about why that situation exists. It is because people no longer trust other people, so they don't open themselves up to others. We walk around with our guard up because many of us have been hurt emotionally or perhaps physically by someone else.

One of the greatest commandments of Jesus Christ was to love one's neighbor as oneself, but his concept had long been lost among most people, including those who claim to believe in God. Satan and his demons convince people that they need only to rely on themselves and they don't need God for anything, they can do it on their own. To accomplish what they want all they need do is betray others through thought or deed, besides they would do it to you, if they had the chance. The golden rule has been abandoned in lieu of; he who has the gold makes the rules.

Sadly, we have created a society where all the values and ideals that our country was built on and that many of us grew up with are no longer being applied to the raising of children. The new generations are evolving in an environment of evil and accepting it. Instead, many growing up today learn their values and morals from the things they see on the internet, movies and television. Their parents are too busy trying to make it in the world and don't have time to spend with their children. Those children learn from what they see and hear, whether it is good or bad.

The workplace used to be a place where a person could go, and they felt safe. That is no longer the case, although there are people who believe they are safe at work. We are constantly hearing stories about a person that loses it at work or experiences some event that causes them to act in a violent way towards co-workers. As if that were not bad enough, many women are subjected to sexual harassment from their co-workers or supervisors. While some women do report these incidents, many others do not report because they are fearful of losing their employment. These too are acts of evil that are committed by people that are supposed to be good people.

The most difficult form of evil to identify is that perpetrated by friends. Not long ago, I spoke with a man who had just found out that his best friend since high school had been having a secret affair with his wife for over five years. He had no idea this was going on and their families had been celebrating holidays and special occasions together during this entire time. He was betrayed by people he trusted, and now two families have been ruined because of the selfishness of these to people to indulge in illicit sexual behavior.

What makes a best friend and trusted spouse betray a person they both cared about in such an evil way? Analysis of the situation can reveal a number of issues, but the reality is that lack of respect for the relationship or the people involved drives much of what happens. Additionally, the people committing this type of act are exercising the worst type of selfishness for their self-gratification.

Chapter Ten

The Church Losing Ground

There is little doubt that attendance and membership in churches are down over the last decade. Not only that, but aslo many churches today are compromising their teachings and beliefs in order to accommodate the growing population of homosexual people that either belong to the church or want to enter the church. Add to this the fact that the Catholic Church has systematically covered up numerous cases of sexual abuse by priests with young boys in various church-sponsored programs.

Once upon a time, not too long ago, the church was a vital part of the community and people not only looked forward to going to church, but it was a focal point in their lives. Despite many people still claiming to be Christians, less than twenty percent of those claiming this affiliation attend church regularly or lead their lives according to biblical principles. When asked, people give the following response to why they no longer attend church. "The teachings are not relevant to my life today, I believe God no longer cares about me, it is a waste of time, and the people attending church are hypocrites." These are just a few of the reasons given, there are, of course, many more.

Why do people feel this way about the church? Perhaps it is because the mainstream media does not promote anything that is related to God or Jesus Christ. If anything, they discourage any discussion along these lines, and they certainly don't run any stories related to God. They do, however, jump on all opportunities to promote a negative story and criticize those that support any Christian beliefs.

The church is not dying, but the congregations are steadily losing their way or seeking alternatives to church attendance. Many churches are still unwilling to engage prospective members via social media and in reality this is the way the younger generation communicates today, so they must get over the hesitation to engage these younger individuals. Many people attend church because they feel comfortable with the leadership of that church, but it the leadership changes or they do something the members don't agree with, they leave that church. There are lots of churches out there, and they are all competing for the same pool of potential members.

Many churches proclaim that everyone is welcome at the house of God, yet when looking at the congregation, you will find that it is made up of specific types of people. You may, for example, see few, if any, mixed couples, or young people and those in attendance look suspiciously at strangers. Old line churches are made up of senior citizens that have been at the same church for decades. The children of those individuals have grown up and moved away and most no longer attend church services.

Recently I visited my father who still lives in the same neighborhood that I grew up in fifty years ago. Today the neighborhood is made up of old houses and old people; no children live there anymore and churches follow that same model. The local Catholic Church congregation has steadily lost parishioners through attrition, death, illness and lack of interest. When I was growing up and attending that same church, it was always full in

Sunday mass, today, it is about half full for most masses. Sadly, the church is doing little to attract of draw in new parishioners.

Perhaps what is causing the greatest loss of membership in church attendance is the push towards self-awareness of human abilities. If people are convinced that they can accomplish anything they want on their own, they conclude that there is no need for spiritual intervention, hence no need to attend church services.

Chapter Eleven

Destruction of the Family: Evil at the Core

The family as we used to know it is in the process of being destroyed every day. The divorce rate is higher that it has ever been, and there are children being born every day who have no idea who their father might be. As if that wasn't bad enough, the courts take children away from the only parent they have ever known. The laws that are supposed to be in the best interest of the child seldom are, and the child is placed with strangers. Courts today are quick to jump on any allegation of child abuse regardless of whether it is substantiated or not, whatever happened to good old fashioned discipline? These types of allegations can destroy a parent's reputation and placing the children in foster care does no one any good other than those foster parents that are being paid by the court and many times could care less about the children.

Family members are no longer showing affection towards children because they don't want to be accused of inappropriate behavior. As a result, children today grow up feeling that their family members don't care about them. In time's past, uncles, aunts, grandfathers and grandmothers used to hug and kiss their nieces, nephews, and grandchildren; now they are afraid to touch them because they may be accused of inappropriate touching.

If a disgruntled parent wants to keep a child away from the other parent, all they have to do is get a lawyer. They file a brief with the family court indicating to the judge that the parent is somehow abusing the child. Most likely, the court will issue an order preventing the parent from seeing the child in the future. These types of actions happen in courtrooms all over the country every day. Here is the sad truth based on statistical data: in about 80% of these alleged cases of child abuse, the accusations are false and are made simply as revenge against the parent.

God created the family for a very specific reason. The family is a reflection of God himself since he is our Father and provider. Like a family father, God leads us, corrects us, and protects us. Sadly, many fathers have forgotten that those responsibilities come with the job when God grants them the gift of a family and children. While men tend to be the biggest violators when it comes to abandoning their family, women are not immune and they too sometimes run away from those responsibilities in search of self-gratification. In many homes, we see both parents working hard to further their careers or make ends meet because they are living beyond their means, and the children are raising themselves. Children require the attention and direction of parents in many areas of their lives as they are becoming responsible adults. When children do not get that direction and guidance from their parents, they will seek out others who are willing to provide it.

Some people believe that children can be raised by same-sex parents and that there will be no impact at all on their development. Since there is little evidence or statistical information to dispute this idea, I will not attempt to argue the point. What I will say is, from my personal knowledge, these children miss out on the experiences that can only be provided by a traditional family environment. Some may argue that this is a very subjective view of this topic, and perhaps they are right. My remarks here are based solely on what I have personally observed in these type of family units and the children that are in them. From my viewpoint it is not a healthy environment, whether it is right or wrong is not for me to say and those individuals will have to answer to the Almighty when their time comes.

More and more, we see God being removed from the not only the family, but also from institutions, schools, government buildings, and other public places. Even the mention of anything Godly in the workplace can get a person into serious trouble and threaten their employment. Some schools are now teaching children, with their parent's approval, information regarding alternative sexual lifestyles and the government does nothing to prevent that but mention God and the lawyers come out of the woodwork. Where is this information going to lead these children? Many argue that homosexuality is something that people are born with, which implies that God made these people this way, which it contradictory to what is stated in the Bible about same-sex relations. For better or worse, these people believe that this is the lifestyle they are supposed to lead, and they have to live with that decision, whatever it brings their way.

The family is slowing falling apart, along with all the values and principle upon which our country was founded. In the Bible, the cities of Sodom and Gomorrah were destroyed by God because of their sinful ways. Are we on that same path? I believe we are, and that saddens my heart and mind.

Conclusion

In presenting this information, I have merely scratched the surface the surface of the evils we are facing in our country today. I began by giving a short presentation on how the country has lost its moral compass. In many areas people today are accepting of wrongdoing even though they know it is wrong, but they have let themselves be deceived. For example, the amount of sexual content on television and the subject matter itself, such as same-sex relationships is increasing daily, and no one seems concerned about it. It reminds me of the story of the frog that is put into a pan with cold water and slowly the temperature is raised until the frog is boiled to death, not realizing what happened to it. We are the frog, and temperature is being raised slowly by all the evil that we are allowing into our lives, ultimately we will be boiled to death.

We have seen the media accelerate the speed at which they produce programming that conforms to what the general population is doing. A key example of this is a prime time program where two homosexual men adopt a little girl and are raising her as their own. This program has been fully adopted by the general public and has even given awards for the programming and the roles the actors are playing. A clear example of accepting something that is wrong and claiming it is acceptable and right.

The amount of hate that has surfaced again our country is unprecedented. As of this writing, several police officers were shot in New York City simply because they wore the uniform. Some minority people are taking the law into their hands because they believe the government is no longer protecting them. The growth of white supremacist groups is also at an all-time high and of great concern for law enforcement.

Despite the benefits of the growth of technology, it truly is a double-edged sword. Predators are using the Internet to find victims. These victims are children, the elderly and normal citizens that are scammed out of their hard-earned money. Children are lured by sexual deviants, and many are abused and killed. Women are stalked by men who wish to do them harm.

Because of the ready availability of firearms, many use these firearms to resolve conflicts with deadly consequences. Respect for human life is no longer of concern. Gang violence results in death of many young people that choose that particular lifestyle. Along with this lack of respect for human life by gang members, is the lack of respect for the human fetus' that are aborted every day across the country. This issue is further complicated by the numbers of people that are participating in unprotected sex outside of the marriage covenant.

Our political systems have done little to nothing to stop this onslaught of abortions. If anything, some of the rulings have made it easier, and many politicians support this pro-choice position, including our current president. Today politicians appear to be more interested in setting themselves up for re-election rather than doing what is right in the eyes of God or the best interest of the people. Those politicians that end up in Congress quickly find out that they are powerless to affect change, and they are at the mercy of the bureaucracy that exists in Washington.

For decades, the beauty of America was that not only was it the land of opportunity, but also it was a God-fearing land built on Godly values and strong scriptural principles. That country is now gone. Our currency still says, "In God We Trust," but those are only words on pieces of paper. I believe that in time politicians will find a way to remove those words too from the public eye. People today tend to be out for themselves and helping their neighbor is left to those "goody two shoes," types that are out there, still believe in God and the Ten Commandments.

In the last twenty years, I have seen an unprecedented decline in the traditional family and the role of the church in family life. People in many walks of life have turned their backs on not only the church, but also on God himself. They claim that God and the church are no longer relevant in their lives, and they don't want to waste time there because life is too short. While there is little doubt that there is an increase in all forms of homosexual behavior, much of it has to do with choice and nothing to do with biology. This behavior is now acceptable in most areas of our country, even in our military and the general mass media. Many States have already approved the marriage of same-sex individuals, which simply sanctions the behavior of these individuals.

If you have read through to this final page, I believe you have a much clearer understanding of how powerful Satan's influence is in our country. More importantly, you are concerned about what is happening as well. Our citizens are being seduced into this evil behavior every day by the trappings of the world around them. Every day people are falling prey to the snares of evil, and many do not even realize what is happening. The only way we are going to see our way out of this mess is to turn back to God for help. As a nation, I don't see that happening. Hopefully, if you have read this far, you will take steps to guard your heart and mind, so that you can protect yourself and those you love from the evil that is all around you. Make no mistake about it friends; we are in the greatest spiritual war of our lives. Sadly, too many believers are not taking it seriously and are leaving themselves exposed to the traps and temptations of the devil. Don't ever forget, Satan was once one of God's highest angels with significant powers and intellect, which he is now using against us.

May the strength of Jesus Christ be always at your side and with you, to protect you from the evil of Satan and his demons.

ABOUT THE AUTHOR

Dr. Vigil is an adjunct professor at several universities and is retired from the security industry, having served in several security director positions in private industry and government. He is a retired Federal Agent from the Air Force Office of Special Investigations and has earned graduate degrees in Criminal Justice, Political Science and Public Administration as well as a Doctorate in Business Administration. He is also a former Certified Protection Professional. He writes books on personal growth and development which can be found on Amazon.com. Some of his other works include:

Choose to Believe

If Only I

Pathways to a Better Life

Success Your Way

The Big D's of Life

The Mind Bible

I Still Have Time

2nd Chances

Mixed Bag: Short Essays

100 Ways to Protect Your Family and Yourself From Crime

He can be reached at jvigillv@gmail.com

Printed in Poland
by Amazon Fulfillment
Poland Sp. z o.o., Wrocław

53561381R00027